Empowering Thoughts

The Secret or The Law of Attraction
in
The Torah, Talmud & Zohar

Receive whatever you want !

Rabbi Avraham Tzvi Schwartz

From the author of:

A Handful of Light, The Need to be Great, Keep Smiling, and other works

**MELECH
PUBLICATIONS**
MESHECH CHOCHMA 27/3
MODIIN ELITE 71919 ISRAEL

PUBLISHER'S PREFACE

Give to the world the best you have,
And the best will come back to you.

The old adage that "He profits most who serves best" is no mere altruism.

Look around you. What businesses are going ahead? What men are making the big successes? Are they the ones who grab the passing dollar, careless of what they offer in return? Or are they those who are striving always to give a little greater value, a little more work than they are paid for?

When scales are balanced evenly, a trifle of extra weight thrown into either side overbalances the other as effectively as a ton.

In the same way, a little better value, a little extra effort, makes the man or the business stand out from the great mass of mediocrity like a tall man among pigmies, and brings results out of all proportion to the additional effort involved.

It pays—not merely altruistically, but in good, hard, round dollars—to give a little more value than seems necessary, to work a bit harder than you are paid for. It's that extra ounce of value that counts.

For the law of attraction is service. We receive in proportion as we give out. In fact, we usually receive in far greater proportion.

Back of everything is the immutable law of the Universe—that what you are but the effect. Your thoughts are the causes. The only way you can change the effect is by first changing the cause.

People live in poverty and want because they are so wrapped up in their sufferings that they give out thoughts only of lack and sorrow. They expect want. They open the door of their mind only to hardship and sickness and poverty. True—they hope for something better—but their hopes are so drowned by their fears that they never have a chance.

You cannot receive good while expecting evil. You cannot demonstrate plenty while looking for poverty.

Blessed is he that expecteth much, for verily his soul shall be filled.

"The Secret of Receive whatever you want" or "The Law of Attraction" is not a new concept.

In fact,it isn't a secret at all.

This Secret was first promulgated by some of the earliest wise men, and it appears again and again throughout the Torah,Talmud and Zohar.

But very few people have learned or understand it.

That's why it's unfamiliar to many and the reason it remains virtually a secret.

This work is a collection of pieces on how to receive all we wish to receive – "all" here meaning all! The key lies in holding empowered thoughts in our mind. Such thoughts, in and of themselves, are a type of prayer, and with such prayer we release every type of goodness into our lives; with such mental images we unleash the very power of Creation.

THE PUBLISHER

Contents

Opening Words................................4

See it...5

Think it 12

Aim for it..................................19

Say it..26

Do it...31

Know it 40

Dance of the Threes....................46

Chanukah Gifts 54

Closing Words............................56

Opening Words

We're looking for success; looking all around us; where is it?

We must see that a wall blocks us – blocks us from reaching where we want to get.

There is a wall, but we can pass it by. We might need to tunnel through it or under it. We might need to climb over it. We might need just to wait and hope and pray for an opening to develop.

Whatever it is we need to do, let's do it. Let's not give up too quickly.

This small book is a collection of pieces on how to receive all we wish to receive – "all" here meaning all! The key lies in holding empowered thoughts in our mind. Such thoughts, in and of themselves, are a type of prayer, and with such prayer we release every type of goodness into our lives; with such mental images we unleash the very power of Creation.

Special thanks for those who helped produce it goes to:

R' Yisrael (Ivan) Sacks, R' Abba Silver, Rosally Saltsman, and Chana Yocheved Feldman. May they receive as they have so generously given, many, many times over.

See it

Balls of Fire

Repeating inspiring words empowers us. Similarly, creating different pictures in our minds inspires us.

To see the name of the Creator before our eyes is good advice given to us by our sages.[1] To make this work for us – to make it more real, more electric – depends on us.

We can for instance imagine the letters of this holy name in revolving colors or textures. We can watch it hover over the world, in changing settings, forests, oceans, mountains, valleys.

Then we can envision it embedded in a ball of fire, appearing and disappearing as the flames shoot out. This vision matches the Torah's own imagery that describes the Creator as "a burning fire."[2]

Let's try as an exercise to have such a ball of fire in our minds, allowing it to fill us with light, warmth and lofty aspirations. Let's hold it in our consciousness to such an extent, that we ourselves become balls of fire.

Outside and In

We live in the world around us, and we live in our minds. Our outside world is made of buildings and streets. Our inside world is composed of whatever we imagine, of whatever we want.

---

[1] *Rema, Shulchan Orach, Orach Chaim 1.1.*

[2] *Devarim 4.24.*

Think about it. Within our minds, we can spend one moment trailing through African jungles, and the next climbing the European Alps. We can surround ourselves with marble palaces or green forests, or both. We can listen to crashing waves or symphony orchestras, or both.

This is a power. We need to use it in a powerful way.

Then, as a second step, we can superimpose, super-emboss our inner world on our outer world. We can merge our inner world with our outer world, and have them glisten together with heavenly beauty.

Doing this exercise has a wonderful benefit. For our thoughts, our mind-state and prayer, have a positive, real effect on our physical surroundings. As we picture our world, our lives, so they eventually become.

Perfect

It's perfect, all perfect. It's a beautiful, perfect world – every element of it, every detail, every curve, every shade of color. It's all perfect.

And what of the problems we face? They too are part of the perfection. For, they are our challenge, our greatness. Through facing our problems, we build the world – change it. Through overcoming our problems we are partner to Creation – we too have a share in the world.

We move through our lives from challenge to challenge. Let's enjoy them. Let's smile at them, and turn them into a launching pad for every type of achievement and success.

Three Types

We face three types of problems: our personal problems, other peoples' problems and national problems.

Our personal problems are those we treat most urgently. They set us thinking, worrying, praying – searching up and down for a solution. We do not rest until we first solve even its smallest details. Still, to remain with only our own problems is a mistake.

"One, who seeks relief for his friend when he needs the same thing himself, is answered first."[3]

We need additionally, to make other people's problems our problems. Creation demands that we become problem-solvers. This is the reason there are problems in the first place. Thus, when we are problem-solvers by helping others, our own sufferings falls away.

Likewise, and the more so, with national issues: To involve ourselves with the needs of our community, our people, is to reach magnificent heights. Here, we do not simply react to difficulties that arise. Rather, we ourselves bring up new issues, working creatively to improve our surroundings. We act rather than react. In this, we build up our world.

A Hidden Hunger

We each have a hidden hunger. We may try to suppress it, but this doesn't make the hunger disappear. The only way is to try to satisfy it.

---

[3] *Baba Kama 92a*

Material riches cannot satisfy this hunger. On the contrary, they irritate it, much like the thirsty person who drinks seawater. We have to turn to, link ourselves with, the Source of life. Only then can we begin to satisfy this need.

A 10-yr old has no wish again to be the age of five. An adult has no interest in returning to his childhood. Similarly, one who connects and tastes life in a higher realm will never view his life in the same way again.

The Formula

We come into this world as guests. This world is not our own. As such, we need to behave ourselves. The hotel, which we so enjoy, has rules. The management may keep a low profile, but they enforce their rules strictly and with precision. They reward us when we behave as we should. They punish us for misbehaving.

To improve our lives, to promote our self-growth, we need to learn and know these rules. Then we will avoid doing what we shouldn't be doing, and instead, do what we need to do. We will stay away from the words that we shouldn't be saying, and instead say what we need to say. We will stop thinking thoughts that harm us, and instead generate thoughts that bring goodness into our lives.

To sweeten our lives we must learn the formula; then, do our best to keep to it.

The Way We See

The way we see things makes all the difference. See your happiness and success as coming from the heavens, and it will come from the heavens. See your happiness and success coming from the earth, and you will search for it here on earth.

The Jewish people, wandering in the desert for forty years after leaving Egypt, lived on bread that fell from the heavens. But, you can ask, surely bread that comes from the earth is as much of a miracle? The answer is the above idea. Since they turned their eyes to the heavens, they received their nourishment from the heavens.[4]

Imagine

Here is a marvelous device – worth its weight in real gold. This is, imagine yourself doing good deeds, great deeds. Picture yourself helping others, encouraging them, writing checks for widows, dancing at the weddings of orphans, etc.

Picture yourself praying before the Throne of Glory – drawing down with your prayers, an overflow of goodness, health, happiness – for yourself, your community, your world.

Imagine yourself sitting with history's leading teachers, listening to their lessons, building up your knowledge, absorbing into yourself powerful light and energy. See yourself also, giving over these concepts to others.[5]

---

[4] *Lev Eliyahu, Parshas Va'eira.*

[5] The heavens count a good thought as a deed, and give us credit for it *(Kiddushin 40a).* We normally understand this to mean that if a person intends to do a good deed, and in the end, cannot carry it through, he receives the merit of having done it. However, we can

See yourself doing great things – and turbo charge all that you are.

50-50

It's a 50-50 arrangement. You pay $10, and receive $10 worth of goods. You give, and others in turn, give you. It doesn't matter what you give, your time, your money, your thoughts, prayers, energy – the more you give, the more you receive. Conversely, the less you give, the less you receive.

There's an additional aspect to this idea. We all start life in this world with resources – health, strength, intelligence, imagination, people to help us, etc. With this wealth, we join in with the world around us. However, if we hoard our riches, keeping them only to ourselves, trying to sponge on others without giving anything in return, our wealth shrinks. Even that which was originally ours disappears and ceases to exist. The more we give, the more we receive, and our wealth grows. The less we give, the less we receive, and our wealth shrinks. "...people who take advantage of others[6] and deceive them do not reach

---

likewise explain that it speaks of any and every good thought we have.

Here is a support for this idea. The Torah commands us to sanctify the Creator's name (*Vayikra* 22.32). This means that, even under the threat of death, we should refuse to transgress a cardinal sin. The *No'am Elimelech*, in his *Tzetel Koton*, teaches that when we *imagine* ourselves in such a situation, choosing to enter a burning fire rather than sinning, we receive merit like one who actually fulfilled it.

[6] Literally, bloodthirsty people; the word "*damim*" meaning both blood and money.

even half their days..."[7] Even the half they have, they lose.

Angels

The more we appreciate the Creator and the extent of His doings, the more angels we have to help us. This however, requires the attribute of humility.

We need to remind ourselves that our many abilities and talents are gifts – we didn't create ourselves, and we can never be sure that the strengths we enjoy today, we will still have tomorrow.

Once we see the world from the right perspective, we release tremendous heavenly help – and everything becomes the easier.

Hidden Beauty

Some beauty is obvious; other beauty is less so. Some beauty stands revealed, all can see it; other beauty is latent, hidden, waiting to be exposed.

It is for us to bring out this beauty – the beauty of our surroundings, the beauty that lies within ourselves. How can we do so? – By focusing on the Source of all beauty, and drawing it into our lives.

---

[7] *Tehillim 25.54*

Think it

Dreaming

How high should we dream? What is the maximum we should ask for?

Answer: There is no maximum. If you can see it, it's already a part of your reality. And if it's already yours, you might as well enjoy it.

Enter the world of your dreams. Spend some time there. Take in the sights. Listen to the music. Smell the special fragrances. The more you are there, the more real it becomes – and the more real it becomes, the more it is your life, the more it is who you are.

Dream as high as you can, and make your dream your reality.

Clarity

Dream of being the person you dream of being. And since this is a dream, paint it as richly, magnificently as you can.

Picture yourself as bright and beautiful – as bright and as beautiful as a flower, as the day, as the sky.

Look at yourself as wise – as wise as the libraries of the world, the brilliance of creation, the knowledge of all time.

See yourself as powerful – as powerful as a mountain, as the wind, as the sun.

Imagine having endless access to all wealth, all health, happiness and achievement. You are a part of the Creator, and all of Creation is yours.

Reality

Get real, they tell us, you can't live life in a fantasy. The question is though, what is real and what is fantasy?

Fifty years ago, or even five years ago, many would have said that wood and stones are real; thoughts and dreams are fantasy. Now though, many more will tell you that new scientific discovery has redefined this. Energy creates matter; it is the source of our existence – and dreams and thoughts generate energy. Thus, our dreams and thoughts may well be our reality, while the stone and steel we perceive are no more than imaginings of our minds.

Long before this, the Torah told us, "With wisdom He made the world."[8] Wisdom provides the building blocks of Creation; it generates the energy of the world.

Similarly, let's have our thoughts and dreams create our surroundings. The more powerfully we hold them in our heads, the more quickly and effectively they will turn our lives around.

Insult

How do we respond positively to an insult, and even more so to a perceived insult?

There are three levels:

(1) Respond but do not insult back. Better than this, (2) do not respond at all. And highest of all, (3) Take pleasure in the insult. Look at the insult as a special

---

[8] *Mishle 3.19*

opportunity for you to improve your personal attributes and skills.[9]

To achieve these levels is of course, not easy. Still, we need to remember that such levels exist; we need to think about these levels. For insults are an inevitable part of life, and by handling them effectively, we will manage our emotions and power-drives much better when they next challenge us.

Insulting Others

One response to an insult is this: Ask yourself in which way is it that I insult others.

We have a rule that says that the way you treat your world is the way your world treats you.[10] If then it's not treating you very well for the moment, try to find out what you are doing wrong. This is the first step always to finding a solution to our problems.

Giver

The Creator's ultimate quality is giving. He brings each of us into the world for no charge at all. In addition, He sustains and supports us through the years. The full pleasure of this gift however, can only come through *our* input. We need to unpack this gift. We do this by self-growth, and especially through emulating the Creator.

Our first priority then should be to acquire the quality of giving. We need to give, and, more importantly,

---

[9] Based on *Yoma 23a*, and the Chafetz Chaim's explanation of this teaching.

[10] *Shabbos 105b*

cultivate a desire to give. We need to ask ourselves, how can I benefit the world around me. Or, more accurately, in what way can I improve myself so that others will enjoy and gain even more from me.

Consistent

Our thoughts affect us; they fix for us the type of people we are and become. Therefore, by changing our thoughts, we change ourselves. However, for this to work, our thinking must be consistent.

For as much of our conscious day as we can, we need to plug into happy thoughts, connect to vibrant self-images. We need to train ourselves to hold positive ideas in our minds, until this becomes our habit. Thus, we speed up our self-growth.

Which World?

We live in three worlds, the world of things, the world of people, and the world of concepts.

The world of things is made of buildings, homes, gardens, furniture, cars, clothing, food and drink, etc. The world of people is composed of family, friends, neighbors, workmates, teachers, people who buy from us or sell to us, people we see, people we meet, etc. The world of concepts is the most complex of the three. At one level, it is made of research, exploration, scientific discovery; at another, of social justice, truth and peace; at yet another, of love, awe, joy, etc.

We all live in all three worlds. The question is though, which for us is our main world? In other words, in which of our worlds do we invest our main thrust?

Choose Life

That which is material dies – if not today, then tomorrow. That which is spiritual lives beyond this world; it is eternal, timeless.

Every element in this world is composed of the material and the spiritual. The spiritual is the soul, the life-force of the material being. When we use the elements of this world for a higher cause, we attach ourselves to its spirit and make it a part of our higher selves. We gain for ourselves a share in its life-force.

If however, we use this world purely for physical gratification, we embed our *own* spirituality into that which is material. This damages us, as well as our world.

Big People

Little people busy themselves with little things. Large, important people occupy themselves with large, important things. We are all we do. The more we waste our time, the more we waste ourselves. But when we focus on life's big issues, when we give our minds and hearts to great projects, then we become big people.

Central Interest

What is your central interest? What one thing in your life most concerns you? It is important to identify this; for then, you can focus your efforts on reaching this goal.

Now – a different question – what do you think *should* be your central interest? What one thing should concern you the most?

If you gave the same answer as before, this is excellent. You really are a centered person. If however, you gave a different answer, you have think-work ahead of you. You need somehow to discover that in reaching what you *should* be reaching, you *will* reach what you really want.

For instance, your central interest may be in being a beautiful person, living with a beautiful family, in a beautiful home, etc. At the same time, you realize that your goal should be to increase your spirituality. What you then need is to link the two interests as follows: Understand that coming close to the Creator entitles you to a great blessing, and that this blessing will bring you everything else you could wish for, that beautiful body, beautiful family, beautiful home, etc.

Happy thinking!

Focus

A way to promote your central interest is by connecting all you do, right through your day, to your central interest.

Make your eating, drinking, sleeping, walking, talking satellites to your main goal – i.e. eat that you may have energy to reach your goal; sleep to refresh your body for this same reason, take a break for this reason, etc. This way, your every action, all your energies, move you to the success you want, and you reach it the faster.

In Need or Not

A person, who has all he needs, looks to help others, to boost and encourage them to their own success. Such a person we can call rich.

On the other hand, a person who feels deficient in 101 different ways has no time for others. Before he can service anyone else, he must worry about himself. This person we would say is poor.

Thus, since we decide whether we need things or not – since we determine whether we can give of our time, energy and money to others or not – we likewise define ourselves as being rich or poor.

Aim for it

The Divine Presence within us

One of our main goals is the *Geula*, the re-dedication and salvation of the group to a more elevated lifestyle. This is a time of ultimate peace and contentment, not just for one nation but also for an entire world. An aspect of these days will be the extra loving care we show each other – a care that comes from sincere efforts to benefit and enrich others. However, the biggest prize of such days will be that the *Shechina*, the Divine Presence, will rest on and within us.

"From the moment the Creator made the universe, He yearned strongly to dwell amongst his lower creatures, in just the same way as He dwells amongst his higher creatures."[11]

Right now, we may yet be unable to bring about the grand wish of all Creation. However, we can at least make it happen within ourselves.

By helping others, by being pleasant towards others, by honoring them – and especially with those others who are family members – we bring the *Shechina* into our every day.

By expressing gratitude, sincere, thought-out, heartfelt thanks, we bring the *Shechina* into our own selves.

By learning and thinking deeply about the Creator and His Creation, as deeply as our focus and

---

[11] *Tanchuma Noso 16*

concentration will allow us, we fill our minds and entire beings with the *Shechina*.

Let's then bring more and more *Shechina* into our lives.

Drive and Direction

It's one thing to be empowered, to enjoy healthy energy – to have the money to buy whatever we want and have the strength to run the distance. It's quite another thing to have a set of goals that are worth living for.

A sports car with a muscular engine and sleek lines is useless without a steering wheel. Similarly, all the health and wealth in the world is no good without a worthwhile cause in which to invest it.

You might then say that to have a steering wheel but no car is likewise useless. But this is not true. For, the clearer our mission, the easier we will find the necessary money and energy to reach our goals. The better we envision our ideals, the nearer we come to converting them into our reality.

A Target in Space

If you shoot a target in space, you must shoot straight. The smallest inaccuracy creates the largest of gaps. This is true for self-growth as well.

Now, if we are very close to our goals we can afford to aim casually – from close, our goals are bigger and easier to reach. However, when we aim for a goal that is far away, we need to aim, and keep aiming. As long as we move positively, we must keep our eye on the target. Moreover, just this focus powers our success.

Hang on

Our goals make us beautiful. They give us energy.

A trawler would not drop a net into the ocean if didn't expect to catch fish. Similarly, the upper worlds do not drop a line into our hearts without hoping to catch our life spirit. They tempt our minds with different dreams. When they succeed in hooking us, we benefit as well. Through this connection, every aspect of our lives is elevated.

We need to enter that net, to take a hold of that line. Setting goals helps us to do just so. By putting our minds to our deepest heart-wishes, we hang onto this line, and allow it to pull us upwards.

Duty and Vision

We build our lives with two major elements – duty and vision.

Duty relates to the present. It is all we need to do now, for the Creator, for other people, and for ourselves. It also obligates us to enjoy our lives, to live them with love and respect.

Vision refers to our future. It is the dream towards which we work and move. It also relates to our present. We use it like a paintbrush. With it, we may color all our action, speech and thoughts.[12]

---

[12] Based on *Mesilas Yesharim*, chapter 1, *"Regarding a person's duty in this world."*

Selfless

On the subject of Good and Evil, we know that two extremes exist, absolute good and absolute evil, with a whole range of combinations in-between the two. Likewise, in terms of Selflessness and Selfishness, we understand that two extremes exist, with an entire chain of combinations in-between.

In addition, we see that absolute selfishness is very gross, very lowly. Someone who thinks only about himself, never considering anyone else's needs, is an inferior person – definitely someone we need to avoid.

Accordingly, Selflessness must be the highest of attributes, something lofty, powerful – a quality we attribute to the Creator of all.

Surely, we too then, should add it to our shopping list of personal achievement?

Imagine I

Imagine you know two people, a wonderful man and an equally wonderful woman. You believe strongly that they would make a marvelous couple. However, both of them are shy, and you need to work hard to bring them together. Still, it's worth it. This is Step 1. Step 2 is, once you have danced with the new couple at their wedding, you must disappear and leave them to themselves.

Similarly, we wish to unite the Creator with His people. This is in itself not a simple goal. Still, this goal does deserve special attention. One element that will help us make progress here is selflessness. If we can put our own needs aside, and work towards the goal for a while, we will definitely taste some success.

Imagine II

Imagine you are a woman married to a talented, intelligent man. You sense however, that while he provides you with your physical needs, he is distant from you. How can you draw him closer to yourself? What mistakes are you making to cause him to withdraw?

Now, accordingly, think like this. What mistakes are we making that cause the Creator to withdraw his heavenly inspiration from us? How can we, as individuals, and together as a people, improve ourselves?[13]

Imagine III

Imagine you are a beautiful woman married to a loving man. He cares for you deeply and constantly gives you expensive gifts. Still, you're not happy. What is wrong?

The solution could well be that you are locked within yourself. Your eyes, ears and heart are blocked, and you can't appreciate the kindness of your husband – how deeply he wishes to encourage and build you. Start then to think grateful thoughts, speak out your appreciation – and see the beauty of your marriage.

Now, adapt this parable to reality. The Creator is our dear husband. Still, our negativity forms a barrier that stops us from enjoying His precious gifts. It stops us from realizing the many opportunities every day offers us.

---

[13] The relationship between the Creator and the Jewish people is often compared to that of a husband to his wife.

Filling Up

Some people fill up their cars once a week; others do so more frequently. When it comes to filling up our bodies, most people eat three times a day, and snack in between as well.

We need to remember though, that as we fill up our physical body, so we must fill our spiritual body. To feel spiritually good, intellectually strong, eating three times a day is a minimum, and "snacking" makes it all the better. Feasting on spiritual food, rather than adding weight to our stomach, adds weight to *all we do!* It gives us new ability, vitality and force.

Little and Large

Problems often arise when we abandon the big, important issues in life, and focus instead on the small, petty ones. For instance, we won't give three minutes to our families, but spend hours looking for the right pair of shoes. We gobble down our prayers; then waste hours debating wacky issues. We complain that we're too tired to attend a learning session; then spend hours clutching a novel. This is not good.

True, our minor ambitions, our petty drives and worries capture our imaginations and hearts much more than the big issues, but this is only because we don't invest enough thought into these issues. We must make time to meditate on what is truly precious to us. Then we will live according to our real priorities.

Aim High

Why settle for a drink, when we can have a meal with it?

Why settle for a meal, when we can enjoy it in comfortable surroundings?

Why settle for comfortable surroundings, when we can sit in the home that is ours?

Why settle for our own prosperity and success, when we can envision everyone's prosperity and success?

Why settle for a happy, beautiful world, when we can connect to the Source of all happiness and beauty?

If we're going to strive for something good, we might as well aim for the Highest of the High.

Within us

The presence of the Creator fills all of Creation. Each element testifies to the genius, the beauty and the love of the One who brought them into being. Still, this presence is not obvious to us. Even where we make the effort to see it, at times we see it and at times we don't; some places it is more obvious, others, more obscure.

The place however, where this presence can most easily be recognized is within ourselves. In our deepest thoughts is a glimmer of light that is not us. Rather it is the sheen and glitter of the One who owns all.

We can and must connect to this light.

Say it

POW-words

We can use words, one at a time, to motivate and energize ourselves. Repeating, repeatedly, a single word helps us to focus and even hypnotize ourselves to higher level of consciousness.

Thus, repeating the word "Power" again, and again, when we need to control ourselves, helps us reach greater self-discipline.

Repeating the word "Love" before joining our families readies us to participate in this special occasion in a fuller way.

Repeating words like "Happiness" and "Thank you" when hardships challenge us, encourages us to see the sunny side of a difficult situation.

A second point is that the more enthusiastic we are in saying Pow-words, the better they work. The more concentration and energy we lay on our lips, the faster our results come in.

Jewish Law instructs us to focus on the *ultimate* Pow-word, the Creator's special name.[14] True, we may not pronounce this holy name with our mouths, but we can and should picture it in our minds. Doing this properly leads us to awe-filled, awesome living.

A final point, practically speaking, we cannot stay on one word constantly. We need to use our discretion, and pick additional words to inspire us. For each

---

[14] "I place the Lord before me always" *Tehillim 16.8; Rema, Shulchan Orach, Orach Chaim 1.1.*

moment that challenges us, let's find the matching word, and activate it. Let's say it, for our success.

More on POW-words

What's the difference between meditating and spacing-out? The first is thinking with focus; the second is thinking without focus.

POW-words during our quiet periods, or in a waiting area, at traffic lights, etc. help us keep just such a focus. Moreover, we can use them to create special moods for ourselves...

Repeating over the words like "serene" or "relaxed" help us reach peace of mind. Words like "energized" and "strong", said with enthusiasm, make us feel physically better.

Repeating "majestic" and "magnificent" builds our confidence. "Faithful" and "dedicated" aligns us with our duties in this world.

Words like "efficient" and "productive" save us from wasting our time. "Intelligent" and "sharp" help us to learn well, and steer our life-path with more certainty.

"Attractive" and "magnetic" assist us to interact with others. "Friendly" and "concerned" help us to help them better.

"Affluence" and "blessing" connect us to the world's abundance, while with "appreciation" and "gratitude" we gain access it.

Then there are the very useful words, "help" and "save me". These draw down on us generous heavenly assistance.

Dialogue

We live in an outer world and an inner world. Our outer world is everything around us, people, houses, noise – just the way we know it. Our inner world is the dialogue that runs through our heads. For some, this dialogue takes the form of speaking to ourselves. Better still though, is to carry out this conversation with the Creator of all. We should (1) thank the heavens for all the marvelous details of our lives, and (2) ask for help to reach our dreams and goals.

Furthermore, we should try to link these two worlds. We should see how much our outer experience reflects on our inner reality. We should understand how really all we do and all that happens to us drives us towards our potential.

Thank you

While we speak with the upper worlds, we must take care to give thanks for all *bad* things that happen to us. It's important to realize and acknowledge that whatever occurs in our lives is really, really all for our good.

As painful as it is, as much as we wish to avoid it, as much as we ask for smooth, easy living, we need to accept that each bad event is for our benefit, a special gift to help us reach our potential. Let us give real thought to the details of our world, understand their message and act on it.

Affirmation

Say: I am a source of light – great rays of light shine from me, all around me. I influence others, encourage them to greater achievement, greater happiness.

Say: I am wealthy – I have all that I need and more. I live in beautiful surroundings, surrounded by beautiful people. I try to help others wherever, whenever I can, and the world smiles at me.

Say: I am strong – I have the energy to do whatever I wish to do. I feel good. I am physically, emotionally and spiritually healthy.

Say: I am wise – I look to learn, from all people at all times. I think about the ideas I learn; I use them as building blocks to construct my future goals.

Say: I am humble – I know that my many gifts and talents, my charm and charisma come from the One who creates all life, and I am grateful.

I am a Leopard

Yehuda ben Teima says, "Be fierce as a leopard, light as an eagle, fast as a deer and as strong as a lion...[15]

Say: I am a leopard. I am charged, determined, driven, I am fierce about doing what I need to do.

Say: I am an eagle. I soar high, detached from the pettiness of this world, objective – thus I can see what is right and what is wrong.

---

[15] *Pirkei Avos 5.23*

Say: I am a deer. I move fast, efficiently, free of heaviness, laziness – to finish my projects, to reach the goals I set before myself.

Say: I am a lion. I am fearless, solid, powerful, even-tempered in carrying out my mission – the reason I came into this world.

Focus on the qualities of these creatures, and be them.

From Outside

Detach yourself from yourself. Look at yourself from outside – as a stranger would look at you. Then coach yourself to success.

Do it

Input, Output

We can divide our activities into two – what we do to benefit ourselves, and what we do to benefit others. This we can call input and output.

All business works within these two areas. Input for them includes planning, research, attracting investors, hiring staff, building their assets, etc. Output is producing goods and services, advertising and selling to the public.

Which of these departments gets the most attention? Which one is most critical for the company's success? It depends. Established merchandise needs aggressive marketing and promotion for its financial success. A new product however, requires deep research before it can enter the world.

We likewise should make this calculation. If we feel we are well established, we can allow ourselves to give to others. We can work to promote and sell our services as we strive to help the world. Our main work then will be in mixing with other people.

If however, we still need to grow, we should focus mainly on our input. To improve ourselves is to improve our lifestyle and our world. Therefore, we should invest our energies into our studies; we should learn more deeply, thoroughly, turning our focus to the wellsprings of knowledge.

Input, Output II

Is it right for us to put our energies into building ourselves? Can we place ourselves in ivory towers, dedicating our thoughts simply to self-growth?

On the other hand, if we work mainly for the benefit of others, what happens to our own development?

Both sides have merit. Through helping others, we really promote our own growth. Giving of ourselves makes us more sensitive, openhanded, bighearted people.

Still, and on the other hand, when we build ourselves, others likewise benefit. Picture a beautiful jug – that's you – standing under the tap of a wine barrel, with wine pouring down into it. Surrounding the jug are little glasses. If the jug remains there long enough, eventually it will overflow, and fill all the glasses around it, while remaining full at the same time.[16] In reaching for our perfection, we enrich many, many others. This is the ultimate growth.

Jewish Leadership

Mashiach, the Messiah, a king, Jewish leadership – whatever name we use, the sad truth is we don't

---

[16] When people asked the *Chazon Ish* why he remained unknown for the first fifty years of his life, he gave the above analogy.

To the analogy, he added, "Had the jug however, started giving of itself at an earlier stage, it would have removed itself from under the streaming tap. Moreover, as it poured its wine into the cups around it, gradually it would have emptied out. (*Pe'er HaDor*) May we continue always to grow.

yet have it – not in the way we could have it, not in the way we should have it.

"So," you ask, "what does that have to do with me?" The answer is, everything – and in every possible way. Not only is proper Jewish leadership something that can and should affect our lives profoundly, but we are held responsible and blamed if we don't have it.

"A generation that does not merit the rebuilding of the Temple is the equivalent of one who destroyed it."[17]

The question then should be, "What am I expected to do? How can I change the situation?"

The first thing is we can WANT it. True, we pray for the *Geula*, we ask for rescue from our troubles and pains, we even sing about it. Still, this is not enough. We need to want it and want it.

Now, let's ask ourselves, and continue to ask ourselves, "What can I think, say and do to want *Mashiach* more?"

A Part of the Process

How can we want *Mashiach* more? Most importantly, we must remember that we are a vital part of the process. For, what we really desire is that the *Shechina*, Divine Inspiration, rest on us, and to such a degree, that one of our number stands up with a message motivating the entire Jewish people to positive change.

We have two responsibilities...

---

[17] *Talmud Yerushalmi, Yoma 1.1*

One, we need to elevate ourselves such that more of the Creator, more of the ultimate Creative Force, connects with us, creating a new drive in our lives.

Two, we must strongly desire such leadership, and the challenges that grow from it. We need to be thrilled, even shiver at the idea of the Heavenly Presence entering the world – filling our beings, radiating within us and through us – as we live each day in the best possible way.

Moving On

The coming of the *Geula* – the emergence of the Jewish people as the Creator's ambassadors in this world – starts in our thoughts. We need:

(1) to dream large, compelling dreams, dreams that enter our prayers with colorful force.

(2) to get excited by our wish. In them, we should see prosperity and happiness, the feeling of achievement we want for ourselves. Constantly, we must renew these dreams – that they continue to uplift, exhilarate, intoxicate us.

(3) We must work to incorporate the entire Jewish people and even the welfare and contentment of the whole world into our prayer.

With these steps, we make the *Geula* a reality.

Greater and Greater

Say, "I am Avraham, Yitzchak, Yakov. I am Sara, Rivka, Rochel, Leah. I am Moshe, Aaron, Dovid, Shlomo. I am Miriam, Devora, Esther, Yehudis."

Let these great people live in you and through you. Let all great people live in you and through you. Let their aspirations and dreams be your aspirations and dreams. Let their personality and drive be your personality, and drive. Be them in what you think, say and do.

Say, "I am *Mashiach*." Let the rebuilding of the Jewish people, the gathering-in of our exiles, the renovation of our land be a part of your reality. Live now towards a glorious future.

Say, "I am the Creator." Feel the Creative Force pulsing through you, invigorating you. Let the intelligence of upper worlds flow into you, empowering and guiding you to great achievement.

Destroyer

We need at times to be brutal – to shatter, demolish, exterminate – but only within ourselves.

We have negative thought-patterns, attitudes, attributes – we must destroy them. At times, we speak vile words, do ugly things – we have to eliminate this. With cold eyes, we must examine what is rotten and look to remove it, look to replace it with what is positive and empowering.

We must realize that the negative within us destroys us. It keeps us from reaching all types of magical pleasures, achievements and happiness. It is our largest enemy. We must treat it cruelly. We must destroy the darkness, before it destroys us.

To Impress

We try to impress the people we meet. We may straighten up, paste a smile on our face (or for some people, a scowl) and make the type of conversation we think they want to hear. If we do this to be friendly and kind, that's fine. But if we do it to attract attention, to draw admiration, this is a mistake.

We need to work on being whole people, beautiful people – for our own sake. This means we act the same way whether we're with other people or not. We are ourselves as much in public as in private. To do this, we need to increase our self-confidence. Still, for the quality this adds to our lives, it's well worth the trouble.

At the Root

The best way to tackle a problem is at the root. We need however, to first search for and identify that root.

"...one, who fixes a place for his prayers, has his enemies fall before him."[18] This teaching refers not only to the physical positioning of our bodies, but to the focus of our minds as well.[19] If we can look to the Power of all powers, the Source of all life – if we can see that everything in our world originates from the Creator alone – we connect ourselves to our root, and take an all-important step towards solving our problems.

---

[18] *Brochos 7a*

[19] *Lev Eliyahu, Chochma v'Mussar, Aleph, pg 45*

Only Two Things

We need to be doing no more than two things. One is enjoy this world; two, is build it. To succeed in both these areas, we need *one* vital component. This is to learn. The skills we have acquired in the past are only good together with the skills we learn today.

So the formula is:

1. Learn to enjoy this world, look for ways to appreciate it, to feel grateful for its many pleasures and riches.

2. Learn to add to this world, search out how you can build, renew and improve it. Build it in a physical sense, but more importantly, build it in a spiritual sense. Build not only your house, but your family, your community; build your connection with upper worlds. Turn your world into something sublime and special.

G&R

It's more fun to receive than to give. Still, our focus should be in giving. For that which we receive comes by itself. The only way we control it is by giving – according to what we give, so we receive. This is a rule of the world.

Therefore, instead of worrying about what we receive, let's concern ourselves with giving more. This way we climb continuously without wasting our strengths and resources on expensive pauses.

G&R II

To give adds to our credits. To receive is to cash these credits in.

Which acts are acts of receiving? Which are of giving? Often the only thing that distinguishes the two is intention. We can help someone in a beautiful way, when all along, we are trying to coax from them something for ourselves. On the other hand, we can take with full hands, but really be performing a wondrous act of giving.

Similarly, when it comes to our relationship with the Creator – we can pray for wealth and wisdom, but really be building and promoting the Creator with our prayers – or we can perform explicit commands, and still be aiming purely for personal reward.

Inside or Out

"The show must go on." No matter how great a mess there is backstage, no matter how much chaos, the audience must know nothing of this. They must see a perfect performance. Similarly, no matter how upside-down the kitchen is, the guests at a banquet must not sense it at all. The cooks may be jumping up and down in total frustration, but the waiters must come out with beautiful platters of food, and smiles on their faces to match. What is on the *outside* is what counts.

In the Holy Temple, the opposite was true. The most beautiful fittings, the most exquisite furnishings were on the *inside*. After all, the major reason for the Temple was that the Divine Presence should rest there.

And what of ourselves? – Is it the outside that counts by us, or the inside? Most people are concerned almost solely on building up their material wealth. Alternatively, they focus on impressing others. Aren't these the things that count, they ask themselves. But they are wrong. For we too have the option of drawing the Divine Presence into ourselves -- a spirit of joy, excitement and love – and the more beautiful we are on the inside, the more happiness and success we draw into our lives.

Know it

Super-Solution

We know the ads: "Do you want to lose weight? Do you want to be beautiful? Are you looking for a good job? Do you want to be wealthy? Are you feeling fatigued, weak? Tap into a great source of energy!"

Our teachings likewise point to a solution for such issues. This is *bitachon*, a belief that the upper worlds supply us with whatever we need. If we can want it, see it, believe it – then we can enjoy it as well.

Imagine a ball of fire. Imagine it as a reflection of the Creative Force. See life emanating from its center – beauty, prosperity, health, happiness. Focus on this fire – sense its warmth, energy – the pure, holy Source of all being.

Now, imagine the ball of fire burning within you – gradually healing you of any sickness, connecting your thoughts to higher wisdom and knowledge, energizing and pushing you to every achievement.

Focus on this ball of fire, and enjoy it. Focus on this ball of fire and say thank you. Smile.

Thoughts on High

Movies or light reading may busy our minds, but they mostly keep them in the lower worlds. Dreaming is a powerful device. However, to keep our minds in the upper worlds, dreaming is not enough, certainly not by itself. We need a continuous sustained connection – an ongoing meditation for our self-growth.

Two powerful tools we can use to our advantage are prayer and study. Moreover, they complement each other very well. Through our prayer, we speak with the upper worlds. Through our learning, the upper worlds speak to us. If we can train ourselves to move, and keep moving, from prayer to study, and then from study back to prayer, we attach ourselves to a magical connection that will carry us to new achievement.

Influence

We influence others in a number of ways. One is through speaking to them. Another is with our example. Each of these ways is powerful and important.

However, we can also affect their persons and lives with our spiritual strengths. As we draw heavenly energy down onto ourselves, we can draw it down also on others. Let us look then to see them enthused, enriched, achieving and feeling good, just as we wish on ourselves to be enthused, enriched, achieving and feeling good. This too is within our power.

More Alive

We all have the Source of life within us – otherwise, we wouldn't be living. Instead of walking, talking, thinking, we would just be lumps of meat.

However, we can always be *more* alive than we are right now, more awake, more able – more in touch with ourselves, and others. How? – We can focus *more* on the Source of all life, and raise ourselves to Him.

We can concentrate more on the Generator of all, and draw His strength into the moment.

In Heaven

How do you imagine the upper worlds to be? If you're spending time there every day, in your prayer, with your thoughts and meditations, you should have some sort of picture of what it looks like. Maybe you see great open spaces, glistening lights, a throne of glory...

Here are a few ideas to focus on. The upper worlds contain all life; from there we may draw down energy and strength. The wisdoms of the world originate in the upper worlds; sending our thoughts there, allows us to ask for added insight and intelligence. All charm, beauty, health, wealth comes from the upper worlds; with the right approach we draw more and more of these gifts into our lives.

This being so, it's worth spending time in improving our perception and appreciation of the upper worlds.

Free

We like to think of ourselves as being free. Still, how free are we? In many ways, we are prisoners to our habits – a captive to habits that are not always for our good. A second problem is we spend too long indulging ourselves – looking for what seems will lead us to pleasure. But who dictates that we need these pleasures? Are we slaves to our every urge?

How then are we free? If we decide for ourselves, by ourselves, what is truly good for us – if we investigate our options and weigh them up with our own logic –

if we choose a path that leads to true achievement –
then we can claim to be free.

Equanimity

If a person suddenly receives a large sum of money
– whatever to him is a large sum – understandably,
he feels a great happiness. He will sing through his
next few days. On the other hand, if he loses a great
sum of money, he feels upset, sad, angry, etc.
Everything in his life turns black. But really, the ideal
is to treat both events equally, with calm feelings of
gratitude.

Life is a gift; its difficulties are the spice that makes it
tastier. Practically, it is hard to say thank you for the
sorrows and troubles that challenge us. Still, to remain
assured, serene, happy under *all* circumstances is the
ideal. And, just knowing that this is something to
strive for, can help us ride our challenges to future
success.

The Difference

A heretic/intellectual asked this: What's the
difference between one who believes in the
Creator and one who doesn't? While their lifestyles
may vary, are they really so unlike? The non-believer
lives with his own best interests in mind, and the
believer likewise lives with his own best interests in
mind.

We can extend the question as follows: If one chooses
to follow an exercise and diet routine, but his friend
just couldn't be bothered, he is the richer for his
discipline and hard work. However, his friend, who

doesn't enjoy the same gains, also profits. He continues to eat whatever he fancies, as well as enjoying his extra leisure time. Each one – as he sees it – lives with his own best interest in mind. Are they then different? And likewise, is there a real difference between one who believes in the Creator and one who doesn't?

The answer is that there is a difference, a huge difference. The believer knows that the Creator gives us something greater than a promise of reward and punishment. He has a plan for this world – a project He is systematically developing. This great scheme depends much on us. As such, it is an opportunity. It allows us to be partners in bringing the world to its perfection. As we follow this plan, we create the difference – the difference between Light and Dark, Good and Evil, and even, Life and Death.[20]

Urgent

We have small needs that are big, and big needs that are small. At times, we rush to find – with the urgency of saving a life – some small item. We dream and scheme for some tiny gain. On the other hand, when it comes to great, crucial issues, we treat the matter casually, lazily, almost with indifference.

---

[20] The two main names we use for the Creator reflect this difference. The unutterable name, which we pronounce only as *Adon...* (our Lord) reflects that we are in His service, and working towards bringing the world to the beauty, love and joy that we all so want. *Elokim* (G-d) is the judge who rewards us for our good deeds and punishes us for our ugly ones; this relates more specifically to our self-interests.

Now, if we would handle great matters as being vital, urgent, we would profit twice. One, we would reach our goal twice as fast. Two, we would enhance our relationship with the Creator. For, in pursuing what we really, really want, we come closer to the One who provides us with all we want.

Any Urgent Need

To need something urgently is good, a good tool, but we must use it the right way. For instance, when you very much need a glass of water, you may fill a glass from the tap, or you may pray. If you choose the glass of water, this will instantly remove your thirst. If, however, you choose to pray, you may not quench your thirst so quickly, but your prayer will become the more powerful. Wanting something urgently, wanting a drink, allows you to ask for much more than a glass of water. With your thirst, you can ask for anything you want – and receive your wish as well.

This is one of the devices built into our fast days. Still, you don't need to fast to use it. Any urgent need can help you just as well.

Work, Play

We need to toil. Otherwise, how will we grow? On the other hand, we need to play as well. We need to relax, unwind, to look at the world from a different angle. Still, this play does not need to be a step back. Rather it can enhance our overall growth.

What is the play activity we choose for ourselves? How is it helping us to be more?

Dance of the Threes

Threes

Jt's like RGB, the red-green-blue combination, which, together with dark or light (black and white), make up every color under the sun. Different spiritual energies exist, and for our self-growth and success, we should draw on the energies we most need.

What are these red, green and blue energies?

Red parallels health/wealth. Red is *adom*, which is blood *(dam)*, which we need for good health. Red is wealth, like the red of the rich earth. The word *"damim"* means money; the word *"domeh"* means worth or value.

Green is power, the ability to overcome any obstacle, conquer any opponent. It is the green of growth, of grass, trees reaching for the sun, creepers climbing walls. Green is *yarok*, as in *"va'yairek"*, which means, (1) he urged them [to war]; (2) he armed them [for battle]; (3) he withdrew [his sword].[21]

Blue is wisdom. Blue is *k'chol*, a word form of *ko'ach la'med* or *limud*, the energy of learning. Blue is the ocean, blue is the sky. We refer to the Talmud as an ocean. The Jewish people saw at Mount Sinai that *"underneath His feet was an arrangement of sapphire bricks, pure as the brightness of the heavens"*.[22] Sapphire stone and the heavens are blue.

---

[21] See *Breishis 14.14*, and *Rashi* there.

[22] *Shmos 24.10*

If we tap into these base strengths, we can accomplish anything, and everything.

Three Pillars

The world stands on three pillars. The Jewish people have three fathers. The Creator grants the world three great gifts. These teachings parallel each other.

The world stands on three pillars, Torah wisdom,[23] prayer, and kindness.[24]

The Jewish people have three fathers, Avraham, Yitzchak and Yakov.

The Creator grants the world three gifts, wisdom, power, wealth. Furthermore, if a person gets [even] one of these, he captures the world's highest prize. If he merits wisdom, he receives it all; if he merits power, he receives it all; if merits wealth, he receives it all. When however, is this so? When it comes to him as heaven's gift...[25]

These teachings parallel each other: Avraham is the pillar of kindness – giving to others leads to amassing more wealth. Yitzchak is the pillar of prayer – this leads to self-control and the ability to perform miracles. Yakov is the pillar of Torah wisdom – the ability to peer into the future, and create programs that lead to every type of achievement.

---

[23] Torah wisdom does not declare a monopoly over wisdom, after all the truth is the truth, and anyone is able to discover it. What it does claim is that only it prescribes a full program by which a Jew gains for himself good living in this world, and eternity beyond it.

[24] *Pirkei Avos* 1.2.

[25] *Midrash Tanchuma, Mattos 5.*

Any of these three is a key that opens the world's treasure houses, and grants us our hearts' desires. When used together, they are that much more powerful.

Love, Awe and Joy

In the realm of attributes and attitudes is an important three. These are Love, Awe and Joy.[26]

(1) Love parallels Giving, which in turn leads to health/wealth. (2) Awe parallels Prayer, and therefore the power of self-discipline, as well as drawing down heavenly help and performing of miracles. (3) Joy parallels Wisdom, which creates for us a path to success and achievement.

Along these lines, let's look at another teaching: ...the students of our father Avraham have (1) a generous eye, (2) are not greedy, and (3) are humble ... whereas, the students of the evil Bilaam have a mean eye, are greedy and grasping, and are arrogant ... the first inherit eternity ... the latter are destroyed ... [27]

Having a generous eye parallels Love. Not being greedy and grasping leads to Joy. Being humble in the face of our giant, magnificent universe, allows us to experience feelings of Awe.

---

[26] The acronym for these three words in Hebrew, אהבה - love, יראה - awe, and שמחה - joy, is אי"ש, which indicates a person of importance.

[27] *Pirkei Avos* 5.20

Three Relationships

We enjoy three types of relationships. These are (1) our interaction with other people, (2) our connection with the Creator, and (3) our relationship with ourselves.

These three we can link to the three pillars as follows:

(1) To interact successfully with other people, we should focus on showing Kindness to them, on giving to them.

(2) To connect ourselves with the Creator, our main vehicle is Prayer.

(3) To build our relationship with ourselves, to grow and improve ourselves, depends on Wisdom – on knowing and understanding ourselves.[28]

We can also link these three types of relationships with our three areas of need, (1) our physical needs, (2) our emotional needs, and (3) our intellectual, or spiritual, needs.

By investing energy into the three pillars, we feed and boost our three needs.

Three Crowns

The *Mishna* speaks of three crowns, the crown of Kingship – for those who rule the Jewish people – the crown of the *Kehuna* – for those who perform the temple service – and the crown of Torah – for those who explore the Universe's deepest secrets.[29]

---

[28] Our relationship with ourselves is also a relationship with the Creator, for the soul of a person is "a part of G-d above." (*Iyov 31.2*)

Corresponding this, the Temple had two main sections, the *Kodesh* (the Holy) and the *Kodesh Kadoshim* (the Holy of Holies). In the *Kodesh,* stood three items, the golden table, the golden altar and the golden *menorah.*

The golden table had, worked into its design, a golden crown. This stands for the crown of Kingship and wealth. The golden altar also had a crown; this parallels the crown of the *Kehuna,* and the power of prayer. The golden menorah, which represents wisdom, had no crown. Where was its crown?

In the *Kodesh Kadoshim,* only one item stood. This was the *Aron HaKodesh* (the Holy Ark). It parallels and encompasses all three of the items in the *Kodesh.* Worked into its cover, is a golden crown.

Both the *menorah* and the *Aron HaKodesh* represent Torah wisdom. The *menorah* is wisdom in terms of this world, the world we see with our eyes. The *Aron HaKodesh* however, stands for the fire and energy of the entire Creation. It is the blueprint for the spiritual and physical worlds. To grasp it, we must use only our minds. Its crown, in a sense, is the crown of the *menorah* as well.

Ones and ...

We can't really explore the threes without understanding the ones and twos as well.

One, as we mentioned, is the *Aron HaKodesh.* It represents Torah, which is also one. The greatest One, of course, is the Creator Himself. Then there is another

---

[29] *Pirkei Avos 4.13*

"one"; each individual is also all one. Unlike the animals that were created as male or female, Adam came into the world as a single being. Only later, he was split into two, a man and a woman. Still, essentially and from the start, like the Creator Himself, he remains one.

This places a special obligation on us. We need to feel how special we are, the great creative powers we possess, and how much we can change this world for the good.

Twos

What is two? The Creator, as One, is also All. Still – and to allow us free choice – He created an artificial "other", an "alternative" to Himself. The original other is Darkness. It stands as an opposite to Light.[30] However, all opposites fall into the category of the twos. Thus, for instance, there is life and death, good and evil, compassion and cruelty, knowledge and ignorance, wealth and poverty, heaven and earth, others and myself, etc.

In working with ourselves, it is important to identify the twos – our strengths and our weaknesses; those who help us and those who hinder us; the places we

---

[30] We say in our prayers, *"Yotzer ohr u'borei choshech."* Yotzer ohr, He forms light – in other words, it's already there, but He reshapes it; *"u'borei choshech,"* He creates darkness – darkness is a creation, something from nothing.

This is because essentially, there is no darkness, no evil within the Creator. He has to create an artificial vacuum within Himself for this to exist.

need to reach and the places we need to avoid. This all helps us reach our goals.

Other Numbers

We have a custom to sing at the Pesach Seder a song of numbers. We attribute a special quality to each number from one to thirteen. Thus, four represents the holy mothers, Sara, Rivka, Rachel and Leah; five is the five books of the Torah; six, the six orders of the Talmud; seven, the seven days of the week, etc. The magic of numbers however, does not stop at thirteen.

There are many ways to divide a large cake – it all depends on how many mouths you want to feed. With the Creator and His creation, an infinite number of combinations are possible. Thus, when we face the millions of details of our everyday lives, we should realize the truth – it is all one cake. Everything starts with the Creator who is One. What we need to do then is to see the Creator within every element of the world, for, by attaching ourselves to this thread, we turn the moments of our lives into an exquisite necklace – a glorious garland of achievement and joy.

A Final Three

The search for the threes is a lifetime project, and we need to move on. Still, as a final idea, let us examine this three...

Three times a day we recite a special silent prayer. This prayer too, is made of three: Praise, Request, and Thanks. We should however, use these three not only in prayer, but in everyday life as well.

Praise – to recognize and appreciate the greatness of the Giver – leads to a wondrous Love. We treasure the Giver, and draw closer to Him. This closeness is a source of Wealth.

Request – to strive constantly for new achievements, higher heights – connects us with upper worlds. This seeking allows us to understand better that all help comes from the heavens. It leads to feelings of Awe. Likewise, it empowers us; for, knowing that behind us stands the Force of the Universe, allows us to act without hesitation.

Thanks – like praise, enriches us. The focus here however, is not on the Giver, but on the gift. To know what we have, the resources at our disposal, is Wisdom. When we stop complaining over what we lack, and instead, start using what we have, we become much more effective. We reach for a greater success.

Praise, Request and Thanks are tools we have to build our world – just as we want it to be.

Chanukah Gifts

A Flame

More than preparing lamps, wicks, oil and a suitable place for lighting our lights in the days of Chanukah, we need to prepare our thoughts.

What does this little flame represent for us? Why is it so important? Fire we know provides us with light and warmth. It powers our vehicles and appliances. Where does it fit in with regards to Chanukah?

We know historically, that a great darkness fell on the Jewish people in those days. The light of Chanukah represents a cure for this darkness. Likewise, for us in our hectic lives, it represents a solution to our every problem...

Our Eyes

The holy Temple stood in Yerushalayim for many years. With heaven's help, it will yet again stand tall in Yerushalayim. One way we connect with it is by seeing how it represents the human body and its parts.[31]

A few ideas are as follows:

The fires that burned on the main altar correspond to our stomachs that digest the food we eat, converting it into energy. The hot coals burning the incense on the smaller golden altar correspond with our sense of smell. And the small lights dancing on top of the golden menorah, represent our eyes – our physical

---

[31] *Malbim, Parshas Truma*

eyes, as well as our inner eye – which see and interpret the world around us.

Our eyes show us the beauty of the world. At a deeper level, they show us the beauty of the world's Creator. And at a still deeper level, they show us the special mission our Creator prepares for us. The ability to see this mission lights up our worlds.

Our enemies wish to gouge out our spiritual eyes. With the lights of Chanukah, we protect and heal them.

A Connection

We hear Holocaust stories of Jews sacrificing their lives to light Chanukah candles. More than protecting them, we can say, this light inspired them. It connected them to a source of hope and rescue. It provided them with a rationale to their suffering.

Likewise, for us, the Chanukah lights provide a connection to higher realities. Think of it as a pinprick of light emanating from a place of great light. Through this light, and with prayer, study and thought, we connect and enter worlds of beauty.

Our lives are more materialistic than those who lived in concentration camps. Accordingly, our need to connect with the upper worlds is greater. Let's not wait for troubles before we turn to our Creator.

Closing Words

Keep Asking

ow long should we keep asking, praying for what we want? The answer is simple. We need to keep asking until we have whatever we are asking for, all of it.

We ask for things, and then we get tired. "Maybe I've prayed enough for this," we think to ourselves, "surely I now deserve it." This thought is a mistake, and it leads only to heartbreak.[32]

"But, I'm tired of praying," we complain.

So we can take a break – and during this break let our prayer continue to mature, to bake, like wine in a barrel, like bread in the oven. This too helps our request along, until we are again ready to mouth our wishes.

We need to remember that the rule remains constant: Keep asking until you have whatever you ask for, all of it.[33] Keep asking and *"He will give you your heart's desire, and (help you) fulfill your every plan."*[34]

---

[32] *Brochos 55a*

[33] *...until you have whatever you are asking for* means either you literally get what you ask for, or alternatively, you realize you didn't really need it; you realize that what you have is far greater than that specific request. Either way the same need is fulfilled.

[34] *Tehillim 20.5*

Lightning Source UK Ltd.
Milton Keynes UK
UKOW04f1903291117
313593UK00001B/189/P